JACK T
MUK

By
Mary Kay

M2BN

Published by M2BN Publishing
98 Birkbeck Avenue, Greenford, UB6 8LX
First edition 2007

Copyright

The right of Mary Kay is identified as the author of this book has been reserved.

All rights are reserved. This book cannot be reproduced totally or in part. It is sold subject to the condition that it shall not, by way of trade or otherwise circulated in any form including the e-book, any form of binding or cover other than that in which it is published and it cannot be produced in form of a film or video without the prior agreement of the publisher. This condition is imposed on the subsequent purchaser.

Printed and bound in Great Britain by Fast Print.

ISBN 978-0-9555705-0-6

Book order: order@m2bn.co.uk

To my children B, Dee and Mo, also my late brother Martin for always supporting and believing in me.

CHAPTER ONE

Life at the Homestead

Animals lived side by side with human beings in harmony at a homestead situated at the edge of Mukuyu forest. This was an interesting arrangement, taking into consideration their past history. The homestead was overlooking a large sprawling plain with a river running through it. Both the humans and animals were happy about the step they had taken to live together, and were proud of their relationship. It was not easy for both sides to forget their past differences, but they were eager to live together and make it work. Being at the point where the forest meets the plain, the place was an ideal grazing area for the various animals who had moved to the homestead. Although there was plenty of foliage as well as grass for them to eat at the time, the animals were also trying to adjust to some of the food eaten by humans in order to fit in with their neighbours.

The group of animals involved in this new relationship included Carl the Giraffe and his family. Giraffes are graceful animals, with beautiful brown dotted skins and magnificent long necks. They walk in an elegant fashion and as such it is very easy to identify them from the other animals. Kevin the Elephant and his family were also among the group.

These are massive but gentle animals with tusks made of ivory, which are very precious and much sought after by traders. The rhino's too, with Pharrel as the leader, were part of this arrangement. They have valuable horns that sit above their noses. Also amongst the group was Jack the Hare and his family. Although Jack was smaller than other animals, his intelligence and ability to deal with difficult situations made up for his size. Bonnie the Tortoise was one of the small animals too. Like Jack she was very conscious of her size and what other animals thought about her. Because of that the two animals understood each other and were sympathetic towards each other. Included in the group were zebras, antelopes, wild dogs, hyenas, monkeys, jackals and many other animals.

The group of humans, on the other hand, comprised Mr. Richard Hall, leader of the group against cruelty to animals. He was one of the people who made an agreement with the animals, to move from Mukuyu forest and come to live alongside humans. He thought by doing so the animals would be safe, because it would prevent the poachers from killing them.

Poachers are men who illegally kill animals for financial gain. In the past if any of the humans in the area wanted to go hunting, they had to obtain a permit from the police which showed the number of animals they were allowed to kill. If they were found killing animals without a permit, they would be arrested by the police immediately. However the new agreement between the animals and the humans clearly prohibited hunting in the area.

The other well known person among the humans was Mr. Victor Jones, who was in charge of the youths. Because of his position he had a great deal of influence among young men. Nevertheless, there were other residents in the homestead who thought his work with the youths was actually a cover up for something mysterious he was involved in.

As time went by the animals became familiar with their new environment. They made friends with the humans and were free to move about as they pleased. Their little ones played together and went swimming together. Most of all they loved watching the sunset in the evenings with their new friends, when it was cool and quiet. The view was even more spectacular when a rainbow appeared in the sky with its beautiful colours.

The parents too helped each other with tasks and shared ideas with each other. However, this idyllic situation did not last long. Mysterious things started happening at night. Some members of the animal families were disappearing, and none of the animals had any idea why this was happening to them. Unfortunately some men from the human race were poachers and were involved in such evil and greedy acts, because they wanted to get rich quickly. These callous acts were done so as to obtain meat which was eaten or sold, and those animals with beautiful skins and valuable tusks were sold to the highest bidder. Small animals too were abducted and sold as pets to those who could afford to pay for them.

Traders came from all over the world to buy the animal skins and tusks. Elephant tusks were highly sought after and mostly used to make ornaments, necklaces and bracelets. Some rich people have elephant tusks made into fancy ornaments and other animal skins made into stuffed animals, which they display as decor in their homes. Rhino horns too are in great demand. They are used by herbalists to make powerful medicines, especially in far away places, hence the interest shown by so many people. All the negotiations and purchases with regard to animal products were conducted in secrecy, because the men involved were afraid of what those from the animal rights movement would do once they found out what was happening to the animals. All the group members involved in this illegal business, as well as their customers, were sworn to secrecy.

However it became difficult to keep these things secret for very long. Word started going round and eventually the animals came to learn that their human neighbours were behind the disappearance of their loved ones. The animals could not understand the humans at all, one minute they were friendly and helpful, the next they were merciless and harming the animals. It is important to understand that only a handful of the humans were involved in these evil acts. Humans like Mr. Richard Hall and his group were kind and protective of the animals. But the one thing that angered the animals most when they became aware of what was happening, was that the killings were senseless ones. At times the meat was not even eaten. The poachers only took the skin and tusks and left the meat to rot. There was no justification whatsoever for such actions, they had no regard for the animal families or the orphans left behind.

As time went by and the animals continued to lose their loved ones, they began to ask themselves questions. Standing in groups while talking to each other, the animals looked troubled and bewildered. Trevor the Buffalo could not contain his anxieties any longer, and asked the others with concern, 'How many members of our families have we lost so far?'

'It's difficult to know,' replied Jack the Hare. 'We need to do a head count for us to be completely sure.'

'That bad eh?' commented Trevor.

'I'm afraid so,' responded Jack the Hare, sadly.

'I think Jack is right,' said Jo-Jo the Monkey in support. 'There is need for us to have a complete picture of the situation. This will enable us to provide support for those who are directly affected.'

'What are we going to do with orphans who have lost both parents?' asked Andrew the Zebra.

'We are going to absorb them into our families and give them as much love as possible,' said Bonnie heatedly.

At the end of the exchange, the group of animals moved from family to family to try and find out the number of animals that had been lost. They also wanted to determine why their friends, the humans had suddenly changed and were causing them so much grief. The picture was grim. There were some families who had lost not only one, but two members to the merciless poachers.

The animals began to stop their friendly chats with their human neighbours, and stopped sharing common tasks as they had done previously. Such a state of affairs made the animals feel very uneasy and vulnerable living next to such neighbours. They moved in groups and refused to allow their little ones to play with the human children, because they did not know who to trust. Some men who were close to the animals felt hurt by this change in attitude by their animal friends. They tried to enquire from the animals what the problem was, but none of the animals were willing to disclose any information.

There were rumours going round as to who was responsible for such crimes, but none of the animals were actually sure. The animals knew that there was someone or some people out there, who were aware of what was happening but were unwilling to reveal those who were responsible. Perhaps they were afraid, or probably they even belonged to the group of poachers. Needless to say, such behaviour could not be allowed to go on unheeded. Eventually one night, when their neighbours were asleep, the animals decided to gather at one of the shelters so that they could discuss their future.

Once they were gathered, Kevin the Elephant began by saying,

'We are gathered here because of the sad situation we have found ourselves in.'

He paused for some time, so that he could capture the attention of everyone present. Once he was sure that all the other animals were listening to him, he continued with his speech.

'You are all aware that members of our families have been disappearing, and we do not know why or where they have gone. This cannot be allowed to continue, otherwise the animal family will become extinct.'

'What are we going to do about this situation?' asked Jo-Jo the Monkey.

Jack the Hare said, 'Well! I heard from some reliable sources that Mr. Victor Jones, the man in charge of youths, is at the centre of these acts. Therefore those of you who are friendly with him should be aware, otherwise you will be the next victims.'

'If we know which people are responsible for these crimes,' said Charlie the Lion angrily, 'what are we doing here wasting time talking instead of sorting them out?'

'Those are rumours only, what we desperately need is proof so that these poachers can be stopped,' stated Marco the Jackal.

Before the animals moved here Charlie the Lion was regarded as the King of the animals as well as the King of the Jungle. But by coming to live with men he lost his status among his animal family. As a result he was somewhat bitter against humans, and against his fellow animals who put him in such a position. The other animals too were aware of his feelings. But faced with the present situation, none of them could blame him for his sentiments. Nonetheless, they wanted him to keep his feelings to himself, rather than make others feel responsible for supporting the move.

'Charlie, it is typical of you to think first of violence as a means of settling problems. What you forget is that you are big and powerful and can protect yourself and your family. Have you considered the risk such an action could pose for small animals and their families, or our youngsters for that matter?' asked Marty the Hyena.

'Enough you two,' said Jack the Hare. 'This is no time for you to be bickering with each other. We have a big problem at the moment which requires everyone's attention and input so that we can come up with an urgent and reasonable solution.'

There was a long silence as everyone was thinking of their next move. Carl the Giraffe stood up gracefully and shook the dust from his beautiful skin. He cleared his throat and said in his slow voice,

'Hmm! It appears this arrangement with our neighbours is not working, otherwise we would not have experienced such events. As I see it, the only alternative we have at present is to go back to Mukuyu forest where we came from. I never trusted mankind in the first place.'

Bonnie the Tortoise moved towards the centre so that everyone could see who was speaking. 'I think Carl is right, it has become apparent that we need to move from this place.'

'I thought we had a lot of friends among men?' asked Jo-Jo the Monkey.

'We do Jo-Jo,' said Pharrel the Rhino. 'That is the reason we came here in the first place. With regard to the present problem, we know it is happening but we can't prove it because those involved are clever and devious. Therefore we cannot tell our supporters anything without reliable evidence. Doing so would cause innocent people a lot of harm and suffering and I am quite sure we all wouldn't want that to happen.'

'It is quite impossible for us to identify the poachers or do anything about them because they live among us. As a result they are able to study our habits and movements. This allows them to strike quickly and disappear into the crowd before they can be identified,' explained Jack the hare.

'If moving from this place is what it takes to safeguard our lives then let it be,' said Andrew the Zebra, angrily.

'Well said all of you,' said David the Duicker. 'But in all these discussions today, we seem to have forgotten one important factor, which is our little ones. Since they were born here, how are they going to feel about moving to an area they don't know? Do we tell them before departure or not?'

'Don't you think there is a risk that some of our little ones could unknowingly tell their human friends if they were aware of our plans?' enquired Marco the Jackal.

Charlie the Lion responded to Marco, and said, 'If there is such a risk then we have no choice but to keep the information from them until we are far away from this place.'

That said, the animals wanted each one of them to be involved in making the decision, which they did by casting a vote: those for moving to the forest and those against. In view of the recent events, the animals voted to move back to Mukuyu forest. Since each day they remained in their present environment posed a great risk to their safety, the animals wanted to leave as soon as possible, allowing themselves just enough time to pack their goods.

They quickly packed everything they wanted to take with them, including food and water. It would be a long trek to Mukuyu forest and the animals did not want the youngsters to feel hungry or thirsty on the way, as this could delay their journey. Eventually they left in the middle of the night, moving quietly so as not to wake the sleeping humans.

CHAPTER TWO

A Long Tiring Journey

The younger animals were finding it difficult to understand what was happening. They had been woken in the middle of the night, uprooted from their familiar environment, and taken away from their friends without knowing where or why they were moving.

The journey the animals had embarked on was not easy, especially for small animals like Bonnie, who had to carry their worldly possessions with them. But the animals were patient and they looked out for each other. They had made their decision to move and were in it wholeheartedly, and wanted to reach their destination together.

The animals moved in a single file, keeping the youngsters and the small animals in the middle for protection. The journey was long and tiresome, and by mid morning it had already become extremely hot. The heat continued to intensify as the sun moved higher, which affected the animals and ultimately slowed their progress. They had to stop on several occasions to let everyone have some water to drink.

It was during one of these periods that Kevin the Elephant told the rest of the animals, 'It seems that we are running out of water, and it will soon be dark.'

'What do you suggest we do?' asked Andrew the Zebra.

'I think some of us should make a detour to look for more water, while the others remain here with the young ones. This will ensure that we don't run out of water when darkness falls,' Kevin the Elephant explained.

'I'll take charge of a group and go,' volunteered Pharrel the Rhino.

So the male animals split themselves into two groups. One group went to look for water and the other remained looking after the rest of the animals. They ate some of the food, drank water and sat down to rest. When the group which went to collect water returned, they brought with them some fruits which were shared among all the animals. As soon as the animals finished eating, they set off again on their journey.

Kevin and his elephant family were very helpful with the young ones. Once they noticed that some of them were beginning to tire, the big elephants stopped and rubbed their feet. Then they knelt down and told the little ones to climb on to their backs for a ride. During these rides the elephants played a number of games and tricks with Kevin in the lead. This enabled the youngsters to keep awake and become involved in what was happening. The young animals were having such a good time that they almost forgot their fear. Because they were riding so high they could see a great distance ahead, and explained what they were observing to their friends on foot. They were giggling and calling to each other.

The little animals loved riding on the massive backs of the elephants, who swayed as they moved their trunks from side to side and plodded across stretches of forest. They also enjoyed the scenery, the green trees and beautiful scents of blooming flowers, the birds singing up in the trees and beautiful colored butterflies flying around. This was a wonderful and exciting experience for the young ones and they loved it. The elephants would not put the youngsters down until they were sure they were rested. All this display of kindness and consideration by the elephants showed their gentle side.

Jack pulled Kevin the Elephant aside and said, 'hey man! I just wanted to commend you and your family for the great job you have been doing with the young ones today. You really made their day. I don't know what we could have done without you.'

'Forget it man, it was nothing,' responded Kevin.

'Not at all, it was simply wholesome. It seems you don't only have a big body, but a big heart as well,' continued Jack the Hare with his praises.

'Hey man, it's cool,' said Kevin the Elephant, winking his eye happily, at the same time clasping Jack's hand with his trunk.

The animals forged on with their journey until dusk when they decided to rest for the night.

'This is a good spot,' said Jack the Hare, putting down the load of goods and water he was carrying on his shoulder. 'I suggest the male animals clear the area and the young ones can go and bring some firewood so that we can light up a fire. Youngsters, please mind how you go!' He shouted to them. 'Move in pairs as we don't know who is out there.'

The area was cleared, and when the young ones returned with firewood, a warm cozy fire was soon lit. The female animals prepared the food and then they all sat down to have their meal. Since there were a lot of trees some animals, like Carl the Giraffe, had some foliage from the trees as their supper. The male animals moved away from the fire to discuss further plans for the night.

'In view of the fact that we are running away from the humans, and more especially the poachers, we need to take extra precautions for the night,' said Andrew the Zebra. 'We need to take turns in keeping watch for the safety of our families, rather than be caught unaware. We should do this in pairs just in case one falls asleep during the vigil.'

'Well, that sounds reasonable enough,' commented Marty the Hyena. 'Are there more ideas or suggestions from anybody? If not then we had better retire for the night as we have another busy day ahead of us tomorrow. Please make sure the young ones and the females are in the middle of the circle when we sleep,' he reminded the others.

The animals were tired from the journey, and as a result they slept soundlessly. Even those who were keeping watch changed their shifts quietly without waking the others up. They woke up early the following day before the sun was up, to enable themselves to cover as much of the journey as possible before it became too hot.

Charlie the Lion asked the others, 'How far do you want us to go in this forest?'

'Taking into consideration the reason we find ourselves here, I would say it is better to keep as much distance as possible between us and mankind,' said Jack the Hare.

'I strongly agree with you Jack, which is not usually the case between us,' said Bonnie the Tortoise, breathing heavily as she tried to keep up with the others. 'Anyway, there is need for us to move on to a place deep within the forest where food and water will be easily accessible, and where man will be easily identified should he try to look for us.'

'Do you know why we always disagree with each other Bonnie?' asked Jack the Hare.

'Well, tell me since you seem to know everything' answered Bonnie the Tortoise, indignantly.

'You see what I mean?' commented Jack the Hare. 'You always try to be controlling and persuade others to do things your way.'

'Ouch! That really hurt, Jack. I do not try to be controlling. I am just confident and make sure my views are heard,' said Bonnie the Tortoise convincingly.

'Jack I don't think that was a fair comment to make,' warned Jo-Jo the Monkey. 'If we have to work and live together we have to respect each other's contribution, and listen to one another.'

Jack the Hare felt embarrassed by these comments because at that moment every one was looking at him and waiting to hear what he had to say. He responded by saying meekly, 'I am sorry Bonnie, I was out of order, I did not mean to humiliate you really.'

The apology surprised Bonnie. This was the first time she had heard him admit that he was wrong and actually apologise. Bonnie could not help but smirk. Jack was a strange character to those who did not know him. He appeared to be tough on the surface, but deep down he was soft and caring. He looked out for the less fortunate ones, which is why Bonnie understood him very well. They shared the same concerns. Being small in size, the other animals sometimes did not listen to their points of view, and often undermined them. Therefore Jack drew attention to himself by being either extremely nice, or extremely outrageous. At times he would do something to appear clever to the other animals, just to prove that despite his size he was just as smart as them.

At midday they stopped again to have some food and water. They allowed the young-ones enough time to rest, and then continued with the journey. That evening the animals reached a very beautiful plain area in the middle of Mukuyu forest which was suitable for grazing. The surrounding trees weren't as tall and from where they stood they could clearly see the Liberty hills. Every one of them agreed that the area was beautiful and the scenery was unbelievable, especially the red light on the horizon. The young ones became excited because they had never seen such a magnificent view before. It was a truly beautiful view of the sunset. All the animals decided to settle down here for the night, tired but happy.

CHAPTER THREE

Mukuyu Forest

The animals decided to settle on top of Liberty Hills in Mukuyu forest. The surrounding area was covered with trees, shrubs and grass, and down the slope the landscape was also covered with shrubs, scattered trees, rocks and a cave whose entrance was obscured by a huge fallen tree. From the top of the hills the animals could look over the huge forest and more importantly were able to see whoever was approaching.

At the foot of the hills there was a river which the animals used for drinking water and to have a dip when it was very hot. The source of the river was up on the north side of the Liberty hills. The young animals loved going to the river with their parents, because it gave them an opportunity to play and splash in the water. They didn't have the opportunity to play in the water when they lived with humans: if they attempted to do so, humans would complain that they were making the water dirty. Coming to Mukuyu forest therefore seemed like a blessing in disguise. They had come back home to the Animal Kingdom, where they belonged, and where they regained their freedom.

Liberty hills was a large area steeped in rich history. It had been said that it was on these hills that the old feud between humans and animals was put to rest. The animals settled in groups around the hills according to their breed. This was a good habitat for them.

They had everything they needed for survival, like water, food and fresh air free from pollution. The animals slept in the open because there were no shelters in the forest. This was a new and unique experience for the young animals. Sleeping in this way the little ones were able to watch the moon above the trees and the stars of different sizes and brightness up in the sky. They could also watch the sunrise, which awoke them to a fresh and new day.

It was during this period that the big animals taught the little ones the names of the stars and told wonderful old stories about their life in the forest before they moved to live with humans. They also learnt how to look for food and how to survive in the forest. The young animals accepted this change in their lives without question, which was a relief to their parents. Sometimes the animals sat together to talk about how fortunate they were to come back home to Mukuyu forest. They also discussed their life with men.

Andrew the Zebra got up and stretched lazily. 'Hmm!' he breathed in fresh air and then continued dreamily, as if he was talking to himself. 'This is really a splendid place to raise one's children.'

'It is, isn't it?' responded Trevor the Buffalo. 'Look at the magnificent scenery around us. We could not have asked for a better place.'

Pharrel the Rhino asked the others, 'Do you regret us going to live with humans?'

'Do you?' asked Samuel the Impala in return.

'To be honest, I have mixed feelings,' responded Pharrel the Rhino.

'I for one don't,' said Bonnie the Tortoise, 'because if we hadn't gone we would always be asking ourselves what if? And we wouldn't have an answer to that question. When you travel you learn a lot and become open minded.'

'I think you are right Bonnie,' said Jack the Hare in earnest. 'We have had a good experience and we have learnt a lot from the humans. But there were also bad things we experienced at the hands of the humans, especially the one important factor which made us come here.'

'I don't think it is healthy to dwell on such painful memories,' Kevin the Elephant reminded the other animals.

Only rarely did they think back to the time when they lived with the humans, because they could only recall bad memories towards the end of their stay. Most of the time they didn't even want to think about it, because they had moved on and were happy.

Their happiness didn't last long in the Animal Kingdom. The animals began to experience the same problems with one of their own. Charlie the Lion, who was one of the big animals, began to waylay the other animals for the purpose of killing them for food. The rest of the animals could not understand his behaviour. The lion was regarded as the King of the Jungle, and as such the other animals expected him to protect them. The Charlie they knew while they were living next to men was not the Charlie they were seeing at that moment. Back then he was caring for his animal folk, making sure they had enough food and other basic needs.

Having come this far the animals did not expect one of their own to betray and exploit the whole animal population. As a result they felt very disappointed in him. Such experiences hardened the animals. They decided to come together and make a plan to protect themselves against their common enemy, the lion. Charlie the Lion was not invited or made aware of the meeting. It was held in the evening when it was cool and when all the animals were supposed to be in their own living patches.

Jack the Hare spoke first, 'The only way I think we can try and solve our problem, is by moving in groups.'

Some of the animals were not sure how this was going to help them, therefore they asked Jack.

'How is moving in groups going to stop the lion from killing us?' asked Jo-Jo the Monkey with concern.

'It will enable us to fight Charlie as a group instead of tackling him individually. The groups will be composed of both big and small animals, so that the big ones can protect the small ones.' Jack the Hare continued to explain the plan in detail to the others.

Bonnie the Tortoise was not totally convinced with Jack's explanation. She expressed her concern by saying, 'It is very well for some of you to say we should move in groups, but look at me and my family, we are short and slow in walking. How are we going to keep pace with the big animals? I am quite sure we will be his next victims because we can hardly run.'

The other animals tried their best to reassure Bonnie the tortoise. Samuel the Impala told Bonnie earnestly, 'Look! We are all in this together. Should Charlie the Lion try to attack us, I for one will use my sharp horns on him. I'm also sure that others here among us will do whatever is possible to protect us all.'

'Yeah! Yeah!' they all shouted together.

Such re-assurances and commitments from the large members of the animal family united them all, and made them feel secure.

'Do you think Charlie learnt such habits from mankind?' asked Thomas the wild dog, in desperation. 'If we had not moved to live with them none of this would be happening.'

'That's rubbish,' responded Pharrel the Rhino. 'Charlie is Charlie and I don't think he will ever change. He is set in his own ways.'

'We have a real problem here and it would be helpful if we kept watch on Charlie the Lion's movements,' suggested Jo-Jo the Monkey. 'Those of us who are able to climb trees should take on the task of observing his activities, and inform the others so that we keep out of his reach.'

'These plans can only be effective if we all work together, if we fail to do so then we will remain his prey forever,' said Andrew the Giraffe seriously.

'Well that should be the responsibility of each and every one of us, to play their part so as to ensure that our plan works,' stated Oliver the antelope.

The other animals nodded in agreement. Later the animals divided themselves into groups in which they would move around. Meanwhile, Jo-Jo the Monkey and the other animals that could climb trees left the team so that they could discus how to go about their task. They were all serious about it because they wanted to put an end to Charlie's brutality.

The animals went on with their daily lives, at the same time following their plans as agreed at the meeting. Most of the animals knew Charlie the Lion was bigger than them and therefore decided to keep out of his reach. Jo-Jo the Monkey and his mates kept up their part of the bargain.

They were able to monitor Charlie the Lion's movements and report to the others without him being aware of their presence. Given such a good working relationship and good communication, the animals managed to avoid contact with Charlie.

At the same time, Charlie the Lion was surprised that he didn't seem to meet or see the other animals as much as he used to. His food had run out and he needed to hunt more animals. He thought that since he was back home at Mukuyu forest, he could do whatever he pleased. But each time he went to the river he found none of the other animals there. He tried hiding in the bushes near the river while awaiting their arrival, yet nothing happened.

Eventually he realised that the other animals were avoiding him because he had been hunting them. Charlie the lion wondered what else he could do to attract other animals. He told himself to think of something fast, otherwise he would die of starvation. He suddenly thought he had a very good idea. He decided he would make a water hole on the hills near his home. Although the water hole would not be as big as the river, it would allow the animals and their families to come and drink water nearby. This was particularly handy as it would save them the trouble of travelling downhill to the river each morning. He believed that when the water hole was dug, he would be able to catch animals as they came to drink water. He worked as quickly as possible because his life depended on it. He avoided taking too many breaks so that he could finish early.

It seemed that Charlie was driven only by the desire to have meat. Given his size and strength he was able to quickly dig the water hole, and he was happy and relieved when he finished a day later. Charlie the Lion then waited patiently for his plan to work. 'Now the rest of the animals needed to find out about the water hole,' he thought.

Jack the Hare and the other animals were curious about what Charlie was up to.

'Charlie has been very quiet, do you think he has given up?' asked Jack, expressing his feelings to the others.

'Are you joking, Charlie is not the type to give up easily,' responded Bonnie the Tortoise.

'Then what is he up to?' enquired Marty the Hyena.

'Planning his next step I'm quite sure,' said Andrew the Zebra, anxiously.

'Look, all this uncertainty is adding to our stress levels which is not healthy at all,' moaned Marco the Jackal.

'There is need for us to know what is going on with Charlie, and I'm going to his place to find out one way or another,' volunteered Jack the Hare.

'We can't let you go there alone. Some of us will accompany you. This is a problem for all of us and we can't let one individual fight it alone,' said Carl the Giraffe, quietly but convincingly.

'It's risky if we go in a group,' replied Jack the Hare, as he tried to explain to the other animals in a serious way. 'I know how his mind works and can tell when he is about to attack. Not all of us can do that. Therefore it would be difficult to ensure the safety of everyone in the group.'

The other animals were aware of the risk, but wanted to go in a group and support each other. Jack left soon after that chat. To avoid being noticed he moved quietly and cautiously through the bushes until he eventually reached a small clearing. Jack noticed the water hole that Charlie the Lion had dug and immediately realised his motives. He then looked around him but could not see Charlie. Jack sat down on a boulder hoping to see Charlie so that he could have a few words with him, but the lion was nowhere to be seen. Jack knew that Charlie was not very far and he needed something interesting to draw him out of wherever he was hiding. He decided to do something to attract Charlie's attention.

'Can anybody help me please?' shouted Jack at the top of his voice. 'My friend David the Duiker is stuck in the water hole and I can't pull him out.'

When Charlie the Lion heard Jack's call he thought 'Goodness me, my plans are working just as I expected.' He then came out of hiding, thinking he had earned some food for himself.

'Hi Jack, what brings you to this part of the hills?' he asked, whilst moving towards the water hole.

'I was taking a short cut down to the stream when I came across this water hole,' Jack informed Charlie.

'And where is David the Duiker?' asked Charlie, looking very pleased with Jack.

'David is not here. I just made out that story so that you would come out of hiding. I want to talk to you.'

'What about?' asked Charlie, a bit put off.

Jack realised that he needed to keep Charlie talking in order to find out what he needed.

'I wonder who made this water hole? Whoever it was, they must be very considerate to have placed it in such an ideal place,' said Jack.

'Why do you want to know Jack? Curiosity killed the cat,' responded Charlie smugly.

'Well! I was wondering if all the animals were free to use the water hole, in which case I could tell the others when I see them next,' explained Jack.

'Of course,' said Charlie in a very excited voice. 'All the animals are free to use it, and Jack don't forget to pass on that information to the others.'

Jack was trying to find out why Charlie had made the water hole, because he was suspicious of his motives. He could not believe that Charlie was still set on his idea of slaughtering other animals. Charlie had difficulty finding animals to kill because they were all avoiding him. This bothered him a lot, and he continued with his hunt for the other animals.

During the conversation, Jack made sure there was plenty of distance between him and Charlie. In view of his past actions Jack could not trust Charlie with his life or that of the other animals. Therefore, when Charlie asked him to let the other animals know that they could use the water hole, he replied saying heatedly, 'Certainly not, that is the last thing I would do to my brothers and sisters. How do you expect us to forget all that has happened? Instead I'm going to warn them against using it, and keep as much distance from you as possible.'

Charlie said to him, 'I don't think they will believe you, Jack.'

'Well, we will see about that,' said Jack angrily, at the same time stepping further and further away from Charlie. Once he was out of sight he ran as fast as he could, so that he could warn the other animals about Charlie's plan. He headed down hill to the river, which was the only place where he was likely to find a large number of animals relaxing. When he reached the river he found a good number of them, as he had expected. Some were playing with their little ones in the water and others were standing around in groups chatting. He invited them to gather around and listen to what he had to say.

Before he could say anything, Pharrel the Rhino spoke. 'You look troubled Jack, what seems to be the problem with you today? Was your mission not successful?'

'You will be troubled too, once you hear what I have to say! I bring sad news to you. Our so called 'friend' Charlie the Lion has made a water hole, hoping that some of us will go and drink from there. It's a trap. If we approach it then he will have an opportunity to kill us, one by one,' Jack informed them.

'I can't believe this!' said Marco the Jackal, sadly. 'I was beginning to think that Charlie had learnt his lesson. After our community isolated him, I was convinced that he would not try to harm us anymore.

'Do you mean to say you all believe what Jack is saying? How is it that he is the only one among us who has discovered this water hole?' argued Marco the Jackal.

'Because he has been where you have never been, silly! What is wrong with you? You know that Charlie is capable of hurting us,' stated Bonnie the Tortoise with frustration. The other animals just didn't seem to understand their situation.

'That doesn't mean he can boss others and force them to do what he wants. Is that the reason why he didn't want us to accompany him?' said Marco, loudly so that the others could hear him and join his protest.

'Don't be an idiot Marco, I did what I did because I wanted to protect all of us. Anyway, don't say I didn't warn you,' said Jack in exasperation. 'I can only appeal to those of you who value your lives, please don't use that water hole because you will be putting yourselves at risk.'

'Whatever!' exclaimed Marty the Hyena. 'Everyone here is free to do what they want, you don't have to force your ideas on others.'

'Look who's talking! Marty, I expected something better from you. Have you no regard to the fact that you have little ones and it is your responsibility to protect them?' Bonnie reminded him.

'Keep quiet woman, we have had enough of you and your friend here for one day,' responded Marty the Hyena angrily.

'That was rude Marty, you don't talk to ladies like that,' reprimanded Carl the Giraffe angrily.

Bonnie knew it was hopeless and wondered how Jack managed to continue caring for his fellow animals. There could only be one explanation for this: Jack the Hare was very patient with a lot of commitment to the animal cause.

Some of the animals agreed with Jack, but there were others who were not prepared to listen to him because they were in denial. There was nothing more Jack could say. Since he was the first one to become aware of Charlie's plan, he felt it was his responsibility to let the others know.

Despite the attitude of some of the animals, Jack did not give up. He looked at other ways of safeguarding the lives of the animals.

Later that day, he decided to hide in the shrubs on the way to Charlie's new water hole and waited quietly, without moving. Jack was anxious and tense and wanted to go and join the other animals, when suddenly he heard something moving. The sound of snapping twigs made him jump and unnerved him. But he kept quiet and after some time he saw Charlie the Lion creeping around looking for animals to kill. Jack bravely made his stand clear to Charlie and told him to go back to his area. As usual Charlie wanted to attack Jack, but Jack was clever and fast and Charlie could not touch him. However, Jack continued with his quest. Whenever he saw animals going to the water hole he kept warning them, and eventually he did manage to convince the others to keep away.

This was a sad situation. The animals had left the place where they were living side by side with man because they faced danger and had returned to Mukuyu forest because it was their Kingdom. It was a place which they believed could offer them protection. When they first arrived there, they were able to roam freely in the forest, and teach their little ones how to look for food.

The animals were all in agreement in their decision to come back to Mukuyu forest. It stirred in them deep emotions because they were all experiencing the same problems. They began to express how they felt.

Carl the Giraffe told the animals, 'You know what? When we left the humans I had dreams.'

'What kind of dreams Carl?' asked Marty the Hyena.

'About the wonderful happy life we were going to lead in Mukuyu forest,' explained Carl.

'We all had dreams Carl, unfortunately those dreams have not been fulfilled,' said Oliver the Antelope.

'Well comrades, this is a wake up call for us to face reality, and realise that there is need for us to work together to ensure our safety. We should learn to listen to others so that we can overcome the threat we face from Charlie,' Bonnie reminded the rest.

This was a true picture and they had to believe it, whether they liked it or not. There was nothing more to say so they all went to join their families.

CHAPTER FOUR

The Attack

Since his plan with the water hole failed to work, Charlie the Lion decided to follow the animals back to the river. He was not happy with Jack for interfering, and he could not allow such a small animal to wreck his plans. He hid himself in a thick covering of shrubs and grass. This was along the route which the animals used when going down to the river to drink water.

A group of zebras led by Andrew went to the river to drink some water. Because it was a hot day they wanted to spend some time sitting near the river until it became cooler. When they first began to experience problems with Charlie the Lion, the animals had planned to move in groups, with the young ones in the middle and the older ones at the front and rear. This was meant to protect the young ones from Charlie.

As the zebras moved along on their way from the river, they suddenly heard a cry from behind them. They turned round only to find that Charlie was on top of Nicholas, Andrew the Zebra's brother, and he was attacking him. They all rushed forward and began to kick Charlie from left and right, aiming mostly for his head, mouth and the rest of the face. Charlie's attack on Nicholas triggered their rapid and automatic response. Their aim was to save a member of their family from Charlie by whatever means possible.

Charlie the Lion had lost two teeth, he had cuts on his lips and around the mouth. Because of his injuries, he began to feel his energy ebbing away from him. He realised that he would soon feel weak and would not be in a position to defend himself. Though he was hungry and needed food, the pain from the injuries inflicted on him became so severe that he felt as if his head was exploding. As a result he let go of Nicholas on the ground and ran away.

Andrew the Zebra went forward to try and assist his brother. He checked for a pulse, but there was nothing. Then he checked for breathing, but again there was no sign. At this point he panicked and attempted first aid by carrying out mouth to mouth resuscitation, but he failed to bring his brother back to life. At last Andrew turned round to face the rest of the zebra family, and spoke sadly to them.

'I'm sorry, there is nothing we can do now to save my brother because he is …'

Before Andrew could finish the sentence they heard a big gasp from where Nicholas was lying. All the zebras moved towards him and found that he was gasping for air and was alive! Andrew told the others to move backwards, to allow fresh air to get to Nicholas. He then helped his brother sit up. This was to enable Nicholas to breathe better, and he did so after few minutes.

While this was going on, Nicholas' wife and the little ones were crying and were very distressed. The others rallied around them to provide support during this hard time. As soon as he started breathing the whole family was overjoyed and relieved. They waited until Andrew was steady on his feet, before they all retired to their section of the hills.

Word went round to all animals that Charlie had attacked Nicholas the Zebra, and none of them felt safe. They continued moving in groups and were extra careful. The animals were concerned, in particular for the welfare of their little ones and the impact Charlie's actions would have on them. It was difficult to hide the truth from them because Charlie attacked them when they were in a group. The animals became almost obsessed with maintaining their safety. They realised that it was either their lives or that of Charlie, and vowed not to allow him to get away with it.

Jo-Jo the Monkey said to the others, 'The sooner we sort out Charlie, the safer all the animals will be, and then we will be able to roam the forest as we please.'

'You are quite right, but how do we go about it?' asked Marty the Hyena.

'We all know that Charlie is dangerous, but he is only one animal against a group of us,' explained Jack.

'Sometimes I wonder whether Charlie was involved in the killing of the animals when we were living with humans and having those problems,' said Bonnie the Tortoise.

'Give him credit Bonnie, despite what Charlie has been doing to us since we came here, he would not join outside forces to harm us. He was as annoyed as any of us about it,' said David the Duiker.

The following day, as Charlie was prowling around looking for food, he met a family of wild dogs. They had heard about the incident with the zebras. When they noticed wounds around his mouth, they realised that the incident was true and that they too were at risk. Their aim therefore was not to give him a chance but for them to attack first.

Thomas the Wild Dog asked him, 'Charlie, what happened to your mouth? There are cuts and wounds all round it!'

'It's nothing important,' replied Charlie, trying to hide his mouth. 'I was carrying firewood up the Liberty hills when I slipped and came tumbling down the hill, hitting the ground hard and injuring myself in the process,' he added, trying to convince them.

The wild dogs didn't believe him. They had already planned how to deal with him once they came into contact with him. They moved near him and said invitingly, 'We can offer you some medicine which would heal your wounds. But first of all we need to see how extensive and deep the wounds are.'

Charlie moved forward towards the wild dogs. As soon as he was at arms' length the four wild dogs surged towards him and started biting him with their sharp teeth around the mouth, where there were already old wounds. Charlie realised that whatever happened, he was at great risk of sustaining severe injuries if the wild dogs continued to attack him. Therefore he needed to get away from them if he wanted to survive. He eventually managed to free himself and ran away, but they chased him.

As he continued running he met Kevin the Elephant on the way, who stopped him and enquired, 'What is wrong Charlie, you seem to be in such a hurry.'

'Please Kevin, help me' answered Charlie, much to Kevin's surprise. 'I'm being chased by wild dogs and they have bitten me around the mouth as you can see. If they catch me I'm afraid they will kill me.'

'And why are wild dogs chasing you, Charlie?' Kevin asked.

'It is a long story and I don't have time to explain right now,' replied Charlie, at the same time trying to avoid answering Kevin's question.

'Don't worry about the wild dogs, I'll wait here and take care of them,' promised Kevin the Elephant.

'Thank you, I owe you,' said Charlie in appreciation.

'Never mind that,' said Kevin. 'Just get going before I change my mind.'

Charlie set off immediately and Kevin waited patiently for the wild dogs to pass by. While Charlie was talking to Kevin the Elephant, the wild dogs had hidden near the opening of a cave nearby, and were able to hear the discussion between the two big animals. The wild dogs were not in a hurry. Aware that Kevin was waiting for them, they waited and waited until eventually Kevin left. He thought the wild dogs were not going to come his way and therefore no longer a threat to Charlie the Lion. Big animals like Kevin the Elephant and Trevor the Buffalo were safe as far as Charlie was concerned because of their size. He could not attack them because he was not as strong as they were.

As soon as Kevin left, the wild dogs came out of their hiding and followed Charlie. When they found him they all set on him again, biting him all over his body. They were about to tear him apart, when he fell on his knees and pleaded for mercy in a broken voice, 'Please save my life and I'll do anything you want.'

'Shame on you Charlie, why should we save you when you didn't give others that chance before you harmed them,' asked James the Wild Dog, angrily.

'Look, two wrongs don't make a right,' said Charlie.

'That is a bit rich coming from you Charlie,' retorted Thomas the Wild Dog.

Charlie appealed to the dogs. 'Please, I don't mind if you banish me from this area, provided you save my life.'

While they were talking Jack the Hare arrived on the scene. It was only when he drew near that Jack realised what had happened. He was not surprised to find Charlie the Lion in the state he was in, considering what he had been subjecting the other animals to. It was either him or them, and the wild dogs had taken the responsibility to try and remove the danger from all the animals. All the animals in the kingdom were tired of the hide and seek game they were playing with Charlie.

But despite all this, neither the wild dogs nor Jack were willing to witness another death of a member of their family. They wanted to break the cycle of death that had been going on since they began living with humans, and return to normality.

Jack asked the wild dogs, 'What are you going to do with him?'

'You have heard what he has to say,' responded Thomas the Wild Dog. 'What do you think we should do with him?'

'From where I'm standing, I see a broken Charlie. Killing him will serve no purpose, but his going away would be better for everybody,' concluded Jack the Hare.

'So be it then,' said Thomas.

The wild dogs and Jack told Charlie to leave the Liberty hills and Mukuyu forest altogether and never to return. They warned him that, should he be found anywhere in the area, he would be dealt with severely. He was further informed that they were going to send their 'heavies' after him, like Trevor the Buffalo and Pharrel the Rhino, to ensure that he leaves the forest borders.

Charlie said in a low and sad voice, 'Thank you for saving my life and I'm sorry for all the things I did to hurt you. It was actually very selfish of me.'

He then turned and left, limping away in shame with his head down and his tail between his legs. The wild dogs too were about to leave and join their families, when Jack suddenly said, 'Do you think we did the right thing by banning Charlie from the forest?'

'Don't be a hypocrite Jack, you wanted him out of the way just like everyone else. This is survival of the fittest,' exclaimed Thomas the Wild Dog impatiently.

'Don't be annoyed with me, I was just making sure we would not regret the decision we made,' explained Jack the Hare.

'Not at all,' responded Thomas.

The wild dogs left Jack standing where he was and went to join their families. They had carried out their job effectively and were pleased with themselves for having got rid of Charlie the lion from Mukuyu forest.

CHAPTER FIVE

The Struggle for Power

Jack stood, watching Charlie disappear in the distance. He then began plotting.

'What now? What is the next step? This is a tricky situation which needs quick thinking,' he muttered to himself, 'Charlie always misused his position as King of the animals. Now he is gone there is need for a new King, and I feel it is my turn to take over as King. After all, there is no other animal as clever as I am and I have proved it so far.'

Jack thought that the earlier he took over the reigns the better. He therefore decided to send letters to all the animals inviting them to attend a meeting at his home, so that he could announce his intention. He knew it would not be easy and he would face a lot of opposition from other animals, but there was no harm in trying. He decided to use any trick he knew to achieve his aim.

During the time when the animals were experiencing problems with Charlie, some animals like Jack had made their own well near their homes. When the day of the meeting arrived, Jack hid himself in the well. Usually Jack used tricks and manipulation on his fellow animals in order to disorganise them. This was aimed at getting what he wanted, and this was one of those moments. When the animals arrived at his home, they found it empty. The animals were very annoyed with Jack for calling a meeting and then deciding to leave without a word and they all felt that Jack was insensitive to their feelings. They also felt he had been manipulating everyone and taking them for granted. The animals decided to wait and have a showdown with him upon his return.

Marty the Hyena was suspicious and felt that Jack was not very far away. He could be near the well or the nearby bushes. As he walked towards the well, Marty was pricked by a thorn deep in his right foot. He tried to pull it out by himself, but he failed because it was deeply embedded in his foot. There was nothing he could do but sit down, because his foot was so painful.

He called out in distress, 'Please Jo-Jo, I need help. Can you remove this thorn from my foot?'

'If I do remove it, what are you going to give me as payment?' asked Jo-Jo the Monkey.

'I will give you some of my meat,' explained Marty.

'Are you joking? Where are you going to get meat at this time of the day?' asked Jo-Jo in puzzlement, because it was already late in the evening.

Marty said, 'I have got some meat back at my place. Once we are finished here we can go back so that I can give it to you.

Jo-Jo the Monkey knelt near Marty and gave him a stick. 'Here you are,' he said.

'What's this for?' asked Marty, taking the stick handed to him.

'To put between your teeth in case you feel like screaming with pain. I hate it when our male folk become wimpy,' he told him.

'Okay Jo-Jo go ahead, I can't wait any longer, I'm in agony,' he moaned, and at the same time he put the stick between his teeth.

Jo-Jo the Monkey removed the thorn carefully from Marty's foot and handed it over to him to see. Marty seemed uninterested and immediately threw it over his shoulders. As he looked behind to see where the thorn had dropped he saw a huge spider on his tail. Marty panicked, then quickly stood up and limped towards where the other animals had lit a fire. He asked the others to put some embers on the part of his tail where the spider was, so that the fatal spider could be scared off.

The fire trick worked but left Marty's tail burning. He ran around in circles crying, 'ouch! ouch! ouch!'

Suddenly he stopped, changed direction and ran towards the well. When he reached it, he dipped his tail into the water. As soon as he did so Jack the Hare jumped out of the well. He was afraid that he might catch fire from Marty's burning tail.

Immediately the other animals started shouting, 'There he is! There is Jack! Catch him! Catch him! It's time he was taught a lesson.'

'What do you propose we do with him?' asked Carl the Giraffe.

'Jack has been as disruptive as Charlie, therefore he deserves the same fate,' said Thomas the Wild Dog.

Andrew the Zebra said, 'I don't think we are being fair to Jack. If I remember correctly he is the one who warned us about Charlie the Lion and his activities. And how many of us believed him initially? Very few, for that matter.'

Jack was touched by Andrew's support and took this opportunity to make his contribution in the matter. He said meekly to attract more sympathy from his fellow animals, 'Andrew is right, I tried my level best to warn you but no one took me seriously. Look here all of you, I do understand that you are all annoyed with me, but what do you want me to do?'

'Right you are!' exclaimed Marco the Jackal angrily, without giving Jack the chance to finish what he wanted to say.

'You can do whatever you want with me, but don't send me away from this place, the way you banished Charlie,' said Jack the Hare mischievously.

'Well, that is not for you to decide is it!' exclaimed Kevin the Elephant.

'What I really meant to say was, that if you send me away how will you be sure I have actually left? I could be hiding nearby without you being aware of it,' explained Jack.

'Jack is right and knowing him as we do, that is most likely to happen,' stated Bonnie the Tortoise convincingly.

'What should we do with you then?' asked Trevor the Buffalo.

'Put an end to this and kill me, but you should do it jointly and slowly so that you can be sure there is no escape,' suggested Jack the Hare.

'What do you mean by doing it jointly?' asked Jo-Jo the Monkey.

The curiosity and ignorance expressed by the other animals was what Jack had been wishing for. It was the opening he needed to carry out his plan. He replied to Jo-Jo's question stating, 'You should all build a wooden platform together. The height of the platform should be higher than Carl the Giraffe.

Pharrel the Rhino said impatiently, 'You don't always speak straightforward Jack. What is the platform for?'

'After building the platform you should put me on it,' said Jack responding directly to Pharrel's question.

'Then what happens after that?' asked Bonnie the Tortoise.

Jack could feel their anticipation rising higher and higher. He didn't say anything for some time. His eyes darted between the members of the group, deliberately prolonging the tension. Finally, he said, 'Put firewood under the platform, light it so that you can all watch me burn till you are sure I am dead.'

The animals were relieved and at the same time happy with this suggestion. They went about in a hurry collecting firewood and placing it under the platform. Once they felt that they had gathered enough wood, they lit the fire. Jack knew it would take time before the flames reached where he was standing. The animals were all waiting for the fire to get bigger until it engulfed Jack and he finally died. Not all the animals were in favour of Jack dying. Although Jack had friends among the animals, they did not come out in support of him.

Suddenly Jack called for order. He said to all of them in a loud voice,

'Do I have your permission to say my last words before I die, or make my last request?'

'Of course we can't deny you that, because you have a right to do so,' stated Samuel the Impala.

'It is just right and proper that I should at this moment thank all of you gathered here today,' said Jack. 'You have given me the opportunity and honor to lead you as your King by placing me on such a high place.'

Jack was not prepared to leave his children and the rest of his family without a father and breadwinner. He was therefore prepared to do anything he possibly could to save himself. He thought of all the things he had done to safeguard the lives of the other animals as well as his own. Now they all wished him dead.

'Life, yeah! It's tough, what more can one do before he is appreciated by others?' he thought to himself.

Jack wondered why those animals, who thought he had done nothing wrong to deserve a death penalty, did not come out and express their views. It is at such times that one realises who one's friends are and value them.

Jack stood on the platform, looking down at the other animals gathered around him, while waiting for a response to his statement. The animals could not understand such a turn of events. They were annoyed but at the same time there was total confusion. Each one of them was wondering which of them had betrayed the group, by telling Jack the Hare that he should be their King. They looked at each other with suspicion, and then they started quarreling among themselves and shouting at each other.

This was just the reaction that Jack wanted. He wondered how long this chaotic situation would go on for, because he had no idea what to do next. He told himself not to worry but to rely on his instinct.

Eventually Kevin the Elephant decided to take the matter into his hands, because he realised that they were not making any progress. After the events of the day, everyone seemed to be tired and stressed. He moved to the front so that he could address Jack, and everyone made room for him to walk through.

'Jack, can you let us know which one of us proposed you to be our King?' he asked angrily.

'You all did,' responded Jack.

'When did we actually do that? Some of us don't seem to remember,' insisted Kevin.

'You all placed me on the platform willingly without anyone forcing you. You know in our animal culture Kevin, once you put anybody on a higher place than you, it means you have made that person your leader. Since Charlie the lion has left, there was need for a new King and I assume I'm the new King now,' Jack explained.

Kevin the Elephant was very annoyed. He turned round and his face was like thunder, which scared the others. He then started shouting at the other animals, 'What are you all doing gaping at me? Go and get him so that we can kill him off.'

All the animals forged forward to the platform where Jack was standing. As soon as Jack the Hare saw this, he jumped off the platform and ran as fast as he could into the deepest part of the forest. He continued to run without any rest, because he knew that his life depended on getting as far as possible from the other animals.

While running he thought to himself, 'Though I'm a fast runner there are some animals who are as fast if not faster, and might soon catch up with me. I need a plan which will keep them away.'

Jack was aware that because of their size animals such as Pharrel the Rhino and Kevin the Elephant run in a straight line. Therefore it is very difficult for them to turn round at great speed, which meant that Jack was not at risk from these large fierce animals catching him. He was more concerned about the small animals because of their speed.

A few minutes after these thoughts, Jo-Jo the Monkey caught up with him. Jack was not surprised because he knew how fast Jo-Jo could be, jumping from tree to tree and swinging from loose branches. He remembered the time they used to have racing competitions and none of them won a race twice in a row. Even when the animals lived with humans they used to compete, men versus animals. The competition involved adults as well as children. Jack and Jo-Jo had great speed and it enabled the animals to win most of the time. This was one of the highlights of their stay with human beings. As soon as Jack realised that Jo-Jo had caught up with him he stopped.

'Hello Jo-Jo,' he greeted.

'Hello Jack,' greeted Jo-Jo in return. 'What's up?' he asked, after embracing Jack in the usual manner of greeting.

'What do you mean?' enquired Jack the Hare.

'Why have you suddenly stopped?' asked Jo-Jo the Monkey.

'I was expecting you, and since you are now here I had better tell you what I wanted to say all along,' he informed him.

'What is it that you wanted to tell me then?' asked Jo-Jo.

Jack said, 'Listen very carefully Jo-Jo. As you know I'm now the King, therefore I have the power to make you my Prime Minister, and your duties start from now.' He paused to see Jo-Jo's reaction. There was none, and so he continued.

'For your first assignment I want you to wait here. I would like you to form a cabinet and have a group of ministers who will be working with you. Like the old days this will be a group which will govern the animals in our new home.' He waited a while to allow what he had just said to sink in.

He carried on, 'When the next animal reaches you I want you to offer that animal a position, either as your assistant or a minister in your cabinet. And then follow me, but before you leave give similar instructions to that animal. This should go on until all the positions have been filled.'

Jo-Jo could not believe what he was hearing, and was very happy about the position that Jack had given him. He was also proud to be the second powerful animal in the Kingdom. What more could anyone ask for? He thought he owed Jack a lot and was going to carry out his duties as best he could.

Jo-Jo turned to Jack and said, 'Thank you for appointing me as your Prime Minister. I will not let you down,' he promised.

'Are the instructions I have given you clear?' enquired Jack.

'Very clear indeed,' responded Jo-Jo the Monkey.

'I have given you such responsibilities, Jo-Jo, because I trust you,' stated Jack.

'That is news to me,' responded the monkey. 'I didn't think that was your opinion of me,' he continued.

'It is not every day that one tells others how he values or feels about them, but this is one of those rare moments because of the high position I have given you,' said Jack.

Jo-Jo's mouth gaped with surprise until he realised that Jack was still waiting for a response from him. He appeared as if he had just woken from a pleasant dream with a smug smile on his face.

'I'm touched! To be the chosen one among all the animals,' he finally responded.

'Well I'm leaving you now and I will look forward to you joining me later. You'll find me at that large space on the north side of the Liberty Hills,' Jack informed him.

'That will be great. Meanwhile I will wait here for the next animal, offer that animal a position in my cabinet with instructions and then follow you,' said Jo-Jo.

'That's right, and it appears you've got the hang of it now,' Jack commended him.

Jack then left. He hurried on because he did not want one of those who were against him to find him before his plan became a reality. He knew that if most of the animals were given positions of authority in the kingdom, they would support him because they would feel that they had something to gain. Each animal had an equal chance of being offered a position, provided they reached the right place before the others.

The next animal to reach Jo-Jo the Monkey was David the Duiker. When he saw Jo-Jo sitting down he asked with concern, 'What is the problem Jo-Jo, have you hurt yourself?'

'No David I have been waiting for you,' Jo-Jo answered with a smile.

'What for? You seem to be very happy with yourself' David asked.

'Well, I have a message for you from Jack,' explained Jo-Jo.

'Do you mean to say you have seen Jack? Where is he now?' asked David the Duiker.

'Of course I have seen him! Where do you think your message is coming from?' responded Jo-Jo impatiently.

'I wouldn't know would I? How would I know how many of us have passed through here!' he explained in a wounded voice.

Jo-Jo the Monkey relented, and said in a soft voice, 'Jack thinks very highly of you, as a result he told me to offer you a post in the cabinet.'

'Really? A position in cabinet for me, are you sure you heard right?' David continued to ask with excitement.

'As sure as I can be,' stated Jo-Jo. 'Listen carefully to what I'm saying. I am the new Prime Minister and you are going to be the Minister of Defence,' he informed David.

'Wow! That's cool! When do I start and where are we going to work from?' David enquired.

'You start now. Surprised?' asked Jo-Jo.

'Of course I am. Who wouldn't given the circumstances,' said David.

Jo-Jo went on to explain to David the Duiker what to do next. 'I'm going to follow Jack after this conversation. Your duty at present is to wait here as I did. Offer another position to the next animal that reaches you. Explain to the animal, as I did with you, what their next task should be. After that, you must follow us to the large space on the north side of the Liberty hills.'

'I understand you now. Is that all you want me to do?' asked David.

'For now yes, everything will be explained to us once we all join Jack,' said Jo-Jo.

At last he left David and followed Jack to where he was waiting. Meanwhile, David the Duiker waited patiently for the arrival of the next animal. Marty the Hyena arrived next. David greeted him, explained what had happened and then offered him the ministry of Finance. This was repeated over and over until all posts were given away.

The last animal to arrive on the scene was Kevin the Elephant. Once he was told that there were no positions left to offer because he was late he became extremely angry. He stumped his feet in anger. He was in such a foul temper that he started pulling down trees with their roots and destroying the vegetation around them. The other animals stood together on one side shaking, and were afraid of what was going to happen next. Then Kevin turned and charged towards the other animals. Using his long trunk he lifted Thomas the Wild Dog up, twisted him in the air and then threw him as far as he could. Instead of falling to the ground as Kevin intended, Thomas was caught up on a branch of a tree. He was so scared that he began whimpering with fear. He was shaking so much that the branches of the small tree started shaking with him. His family members were scared and they huddled themselves together. They did not know what to do and could not say anything, in case Kevin turned in their direction to hurt them too.

The reason why Kevin was so angry was because small animals were now giving him orders, and because Jack had bestowed the position of King on himself leaving the bigger animals like him out. When Charlie the Lion was banished from Mukuyu forest Kevin thought the other animals would make him the obvious choice for King. He was not aware that there were other animals who were also interested in being the king. What angered him still was the fact that all the positions in the cabinet were taken, mostly by small animals that were fast and reached the place before him.

Kevin continued with his rage and charged towards the other animals. When he reached Bonnie the Tortoise, he was about to lift her when she quickly slid between his legs. She managed to climb up one of his big legs and bit him hard. This surprised Kevin and managed to stop him in his tracks.

'Ouch!' cried Kevin. 'That hurt. What did you do that for?' he snarled.

'Look who's talking? Just look around you and see what you have done. Look at the destruction and fear you have caused,' pointed out Bonnie.

Bonnie's words shook Kevin and made him realise what he had done. He also became aware that being a big animal does not mean that one has more advantages over the small animals, and that each individual animal has its own strengths and the way these are used depends entirely on that animal. He could not believe that he was capable of causing such harm to his fellow animals. He was usually a cool character and could not understand how his anger could overtake his better judgment and allow him to commit such violent acts. Kevin was overcome with remorse and wanted to make amends with his larger animal family.

'I'm sorry, I really don't know what caused me to snap and carry out such gruesome acts,' he apologised.

'Just think of these animals, Kevin. Did they deserve to be harmed and frightened?' asked Bonnie the Tortoise, who was very upset with him.

'There is nothing that I can do or say that can reverse what I have done. What we can do at present is move on, and stop dwelling on the past,' suggested Kevin the Elephant.

'It is easier for you to say that, but can you imagine how I feel knowing that I was almost one of your victims? Look at those families over there, huddled together and frightened. Do they deserve what you have done to their loved ones? That's just unforgivable,' Bonnie expressed her feeling heatedly.

Carl the Giraffe pleaded with other animals and said, 'We need to forgive Kevin if we want to have a fresh start where we plan to settle. If we don't, then such senseless acts as we have seen today will never stop. I don't mean Kevin in particular, but other families who have grievances.'

'And to show how remorseful I am, I'm going to support Jack as our new King,' Kevin stated.

This was the most welcome statement that the other animals had been waiting for. Before they could proceed with their journey, they had a big task to carry out. They realised they had a big responsibility before them: they needed to bury their differences to enable them to get on with a new life. The animals, even the ones he had just attacked, eventually agreed to forgive Kevin. Finally they set off for the north side of the hills where Jack the Hare, their new King, was waiting with his new cabinet.

Since the previous incident, Kevin the Elephant and Bonnie the Tortoise had become good friends. Kevin realised that Bonnie saved him from destroying the things he valued most, which were his animal family, himself and the whole animal kingdom. Therefore he owed a lot to

Bonnie. The animals continued with their journey in silence, each thinking of the events of the day and what could have happened had Bonnie not intervened. They knew they owed their lives to her. It appeared the animals had eventually won, because everyone was on board.

CHAPTER SIX

The Coronation of Jack the Hare

When they reached the large space on the north side of the hills, they found all sorts of food laid out by the other animals who had arrived earlier. Jack the Hare was among them, and when he saw the new arrivals he moved forward to greet them.

'Welcome to you all. I'm sure you are all tired and hungry after travelling all night. Please help yourselves to some food.

They thanked Jack and went on to collect some food for themselves. After that they joined the other animals, sitting in groups eating their food and chatting to each other. Pharrel the Rhino enquired from the others, 'What has been happening here since you arrived?'

'We have been clearing the place, looking for food and relaxing,' reported Andrew the Zebra.

'Is that all?' pressed Pharrel, eager for more information.

'That's all. We could not do much because we were all tired and needed a rest,' concluded Oliver the antelope in support of Andrew.

When they finished eating, those who arrived later went to clean-up and make themselves comfortable. They then joined the others and were ushered to where they were to sit.

After everyone had sat down, Jo-Jo the Monkey went and stood at the front. When he cleared his throat, everyone fell silent and turned their eyes towards him.

'Greetings to you, my dear friends and colleagues. We are at last gathered here today because we have a new King. All of us have gone through many painful experiences. It is time that we put all that to rest and look forward to the new future with our King, Jack the Hare.'

'Here! Here!' said the others in response.

The other animals agreed with Jo-Jo, because they had all been affected either directly or indirectly by the recent events. Looking around at the faces, one could see that there was goodwill among the animals and a desire for a clean start.

Then Kevin the Elephant stood up and said, 'Congratulations Jack and I wish you all the best. I know that is surprising coming from me, but I really mean it. We have come a long way and I am quite sure that each and every one of us is wishing for peace.'

'Well said big man, it is obvious that the most important thing that this Kingdom needs is peace, so that we can move about without fear of being killed,' said Samuel the Impala.

'I know that Jack will be a fair and good King, and will ensure that there is peace and prosperity in this Kingdom,' Bonnie the Tortoise reassured the other animals.

'Thank you for such kind and promising words,' said Jack. 'I know I was not the favourite candidate to be your King. But I didn't want us to take a chance once more with someone who would take advantage of his position and cause us more harm.'

Carl the Giraffe lifted his elegant neck and said, 'There have been many misunderstandings among all of us. Why was this so?' He then answered his own question. 'Because we stopped listening to each other. We began to think of what was right for us as individuals and not what was right for us as a group, and that is what Jack has tried to do all along,' he explained the picture to them as clearly as he saw it.

All the animals nodded their heads in agreement with Carl because they knew it was true. Jack too was aware of this, and knew that the other animals had not listened to him because they underestimated him. He was happy that he took that stand because he had made them realise that being rational and intelligent has nothing to do with one's size.

Jo-Jo the Monkey said, 'I'm sure some of you who remember our history know the reason why we have come to this place. This is where our ancestors used to coronate their Kings and Queens. It is a sacred place for us. The source of the river is found here, and for Jack to become a King he needs to be cleansed here with clean pure water.'

'Can you all see the advantage of coming back home where you have your own beliefs and values and traditional things which have a meaning?' Bonnie questioned the rest of the animal family.

'We can't coronate Jack without having a feast, which was the normal thing around here,' suggested Kevin the Elephant.

'Kevin is right, we need to celebrate,' agreed Pharrel the Rhino. 'And so there is need for planning and preparations.'

Marco the Jackal said, 'I strongly agree with you, this needs proper planning and the involvement of all of us. The feast should be so big that our children will always remember it.'

'Let's write down the list of things to be done and split ourselves into groups to carry out the work,' said Marty the Hyena.

The animals worked fast after that. They prepared a list and split themselves into groups with the female animals agreeing to prepare the food for the feast. Bonnie and Tasha, the wife of Carl the Giraffe, decided to make a cloak for Jack from barks of trees. The two female animals asked Kevin the Elephant to cut a mokudu tree, peel off the bark and give it to them. The mokudu tree was the biggest tree known in Mukuyu Forrest and was the most useful. It is big, hollow in the middle and it usually has a cleft on the side. This enables the small animals to seek shelter if the whether is bad, or if they are being chased by poachers.

As soon as Kevin handed them the mokudu bark they moved to a corner where there were some big stones. They placed the barks on the stones; each of them picked a piece of wood which they used to beat the bark. This technique was used to soften it so that they could stitch it to make a cloak for Jack.

'How long do you think these preparations will take us, Bonnie?' asked Tasha.

'It is hard to tell, but knowing our animal family, if they are set on doing something, they do it with passion and in record time,' responded Bonnie.

'This reminds me of the old times and the way we used to live,' stated Tasha.

Bonnie said with conviction, 'Don't worry Tasha, things are going to change in this Kingdom from now on.'

'How can you tell that?' enquired Tasha.

'Gut instinct,' said Bonnie. 'Not only that, but I trust Jack because he is very honest, and I understand him well.'

'How come?' said Tasha.

'How come what? asked Bonnie. 'You ask too many questions, young lady.'

'I need to ask questions if I am to understand what is happening. We left this place when I was still young, therefore most things appear strange to me' Tasha said in earnest.

'Of course. I was not being insensitive, but some things are better left unsaid,' explained Bonnie.

'Okay, I will leave that for now,' said the young woman, with a glint of mischief in her eyes.

The two female animals continued with their work, but it was getting very hot. They decided to have a break and have a drink of water. Sitting under a tree, they wiped sweat off their faces and drank gulps of water that was brought to them by the young ones. They also discovered that they had developed blisters on their hands, which was a result of beating the bark with pieces of wood. Bonnie was annoyed with herself for forgetting to cover their hands. She poured cold water on their blisters to soothe them, and wrapped Tasha's hands with some of the prepared bark. When she finished she asked her young friend to wrap her hands too in a similar way. After that they stood up and continued with their task.

As soon as the bark became soft, they moved and sat under the shade of a tree where it was cooler. They took out the needles and thread from their small bags and began stitching the pieces of bark into a coat. They talked to each other in low tones as they continued to stitch.

'Ouch!' exclaimed Tasha suddenly, while at the same time shaking her left hand.

'What's the matter?' asked Bonnie.

'I have pricked my thumb with a needle and it is bleeding,' Tasha responded.

'That is nothing to worry about, just put your finger in your mouth and suck off the blood. That will stop the bleeding,' explained Bonnie.

'If you say so,' responded Tasha.

'Look Tasha, we need to complete this task in good time, because Jack has to try it on when we finish. Then we have to make alterations before we can finally say it is completed,' said Bonnie.

'Yes mum,' responded Tasha seriously.

Before Bonnie and Tasha began to stitch the cloak together, they painted the fine pieces of the bark in their bight national colours of green, white and yellow. Green stood for the wild that is the forests and grassy areas in which animals live, and white symbolized peace. They considered peace as the prime factor if a nation has to be successful. Yellow was used to signify enrichment. This included all the food, water and all the resources which were available for their survival.

Other groups too were getting on with their tasks. The ministers were meeting with Jack the Hare to plan how their Kingdom was going to be run for the benefit of all animals. They also looked at their resources and planned how to use them.

Costumes were also being prepared, especially for the little ones and those who were involved in the performances that would take place during the ceremony.

As evening dawned Bonnie remembered one important item they had all forgotten, therefore she went to look for the other animals so that she could remind them of this oversight. She found a number of them talking about what had been done and what was still needed to be done.

'Good, there you all are,' said Bonnie, panting as if she had been running. 'I wanted to talk to you about something of great urgency.'

'What now, Bonnie? Can't you see that we are busy here?' asked Oliver the antelope impatiently.

'Let Bonnie speak. You should learn to be patient at times Oliver,' reprimanded Carl the Giraffe.

Pharrel the Rhino said, 'Bonnie, go ahead and tell us what you came here for, my dear.'

'Well, it appears we forgot a carriage for Jack, and tomorrow is the big day. What are we going to do about it?' she asked in earnest.

'My, we need that if we want Jack's coronation to go with a big bang,' added Marco the Jackal.

'You talk about carriages and this or that,' complained Andrew the Zebra. 'When did we ever use carriages in all our entire history? It appears our stay with humans has influenced us more than we realise.'

'Well let me know one way or the other, are we going to use it or not, and where are we going to find one?' asked Bonnie impatiently.

'Don't worry Bonnie, that is not important for this occasion, because there is already a carriage here in the form of myself,' stated Kevin the Elephant pointing to his trunk and back

'Hmm!' she said, still unconvinced. 'I don't know about that.'

He reassured her, at the same time rolling his eyes from left to right in order to make his point. He continued to say, 'Hello! Don't tell me you have forgotten what we did with the young ones on our way from man's world to Mukuyu forest.'

Everyone laughed at Kevin's attempt at a sense of humor. They were aware that he was trying to make amends for his earlier behaviour, but they also knew that he was not usually a violent person unless he was provoked.

'That's a brilliant idea Kevin,' replied Bonnie. 'Why didn't any of us think of that!' she exclaimed, following his attempts at making everything easy and effortless.

'At moments like this when we are all busy, it is difficult to remember what everyone is capable of doing, unless the individual offers their services,' said Marty the Hyena.

With that issue resolved, the animals left to join their families for the evening meals. Afterwards, they sat in small groups around the fires talking and laughing, and one by one they retired for the night.

It was quiet at night in the forest. At dawn, the birds woke up and began singing and chirping, which woke up the animals. As soon as they realised what day it was, they got up and made the final preparations to the day's events. As the day progressed there was excitement in the air, and the animals in charge of the ceremony rushed around to ensure that everything was ready and in place. The music too was playing softly. This was a coronation, and therefore the animals made sure that the place was well decorated as befitted such an occasion.

The ceremony was scheduled for 13:00 that afternoon. As time for the ceremony drew nearer, the animals gathered to await the arrival of their new King. Jack had already undergone the cleansing session before the crack of dawn. The music was played quietly in the background, when suddenly the tempo of the drums, xylophone and flute increased. The beating of the drums was now much louder and the animals knew what this signified, and they all stood up.

After a few minutes Jack appeared, riding on the back of Kevin the Elephant. He was wearing his beautiful bright coloured cloak, flanked by the Prime Minister Jo-Jo and his cabinet. Being small in stature, these colours made him recognisable even from afar. As soon as they were in full view, Kevin let out a bellow. The other animals clapped and cheered for their new king.

Kevin continued until he reached the area preserved for Jack, Jo-Jo and the ministers. He knelt down and Jack was helped to the ground and directed to his chair. As soon as the ministers had been shown their seats, Kevin moved forward and waited until all the animals had sat down before addressing the crowd.

'Your Majesty, honorable ministers, ladies and gentlemen and families, today is a big day for us, for it is a landmark in our lives. I know I'm the last person you would expect to stand here and address you…' but he was cut short by the response from the other animals.

'What do you mean by that, Kevin?' they asked.

'Look, I don't need to explain anything to you because we are all aware of the things that have happened in the past among us. We have come a long way, through many hardships, but we have managed to overcome them. It's time to move on, hence the reason we are all here today.'

They all nodded their heads in agreement. Pharrel the Rhino started clapping and the rest of the animals too, including Jack, in recognition of what the elephant had said.

'I would like to invite all of you to stand up and drink to the health of our new King, Jack the Hare. Give him three cheers.' Everyone stood up and Kevin went on to say,

'Hip-Hip.'

'Hooray,' they responded, while clapping their hands.

'Again, Hip-Hip,' Kevin invited the crowd.

'Hooray,' the crowd shouted.

'Hip-Hip.'

'Hooray!'

The animals continued to clap their hands for some time, until Kevin urged them to sit down. Once they were seated, Jo-Jo the Monkey stood up and addressed the crowd.

'I'm not going to give a long speech. I'm sure you will agree with me when I say that Kevin has done a good job in organising this feast and I would like to commend him for what he just said. It takes a great man to acknowledge his mistake and actually apologise. I honestly admire him for that. I would also like to take this opportunity to thank all of you for your contribution to the Coronation of our King. I therefore call upon Jack the Hare, the King of our Kingdom.'

They all clapped again as Jack stood up and then the animals became quiet because they were eager to hear his first speech as King.

'Thank you to you all for the work you have done to make this a successful day. I know it took a lot of planning and organising and above all unity and commitment, without which any Kingdom would not succeed. The day has been full of surprises with many new experiences for me. Bearing the above in mind, I now feel more determined than ever to become your king, and make it work. Not as individuals, but together we stand. I should therefore thank all of you for making this possible and making my dream come true.'

He finished talking and he looked round the audience in a way that made every one of them feel connected, as if the message was meant personally for each individual animal. It did indeed appear that Jack the King had connected with his subjects. He sat down finally. Following his speech, there were displays by the little ones such as games and dancing, and there was also a marching procession by the boys' brigade. After the colorful display, the instruments and all the items used were stored away, and everyone sat in their places. A variety of food and drinks were served. The animals had a wonderful feast and they were happy.

At last, the feast was over. The animals bid their King good night and a long life, and began to disperse to their sleeping quarters

The animals enjoyed themselves immensely, and none more so than Jack the Hare. He could not believe that after such a struggle he had finally become a King. Nevertheless he appreciated the support he got from the other animals, more especially from Kevin without whom there would be no peace in the kingdom. He could also not forget his dear friend Bonnie the Tortoise.

While Jack was lost in his thoughts, Jo-Jo the Monkey came round quietly and stood beside him.

'You seem to be deep in thought, I wonder what you are thinking right now? enquired Jo-Jo.

Jack looked at him and smiled broadly. 'You wouldn't like to know about that right now,' responded the new King of the Jungle.

'Never mind that, at least things worked out better that expected,' said Jo-Jo, quietly.

'It definitely did,' beamed Jack the king.

'We took a gamble and it was worth it,' stated Jo-Jo.

The crowd was thinning out. As the animals walked away, it appeared as if they were moving with the sun into the sunset. It was indeed a moving picture. Then the King and the Prime Minister turned and walked away together in deep contentment.